CtA
His Message. Your Mission.

Reflections:

The
WOMAN
GOD
Sees

Devotional Prayer Journal

Angela

King James Version

Jane L. Fryar

The LORD delighteth in thee. Isaiah 62:4

The mission of CTA is to glorify God by providing purposeful products that lift up and encourage the body of Christ—because we love him.

His Message. Your Mission.

Reflections:

The WOMAN GOD Sees

By Jane L. Fryar

Copyright © 2017 CTA, Inc.
1625 Larkin Williams Rd.
Fenton, MO 63026
www.CTAinc.com

Scripture quotations are from the King James Version of the Bible.

ISBN: 978-1-943216-18-5
PRINTED IN THAILAND

Welcome!

Mirror, Mirror, on the wall, who's the fairest of them all?

When we look into the mirror early each morning, most of us already know that "the fairest of them all" will not be gazing back at us. We only hope that we won't be greeted by another new pimple, new wrinkle, new age spot.

Appearances mean a lot in the world around us. In truth, our culture fixates on appearances. Teens post pictures of themselves online, begging others, "Rate me!" The results can prove traumatic—or worse!

Suppose God answered the "rate me" challenge. What would he say? As Christians, we know the answer. Our heavenly Father has already told us we are his unique, dearly loved creations. He made us in his image, and even though sin has marred and disfigured us, our Lord still sees us as holy, flawless, beautiful. We have his word on that.

We are not now what we should be. We are not yet all we will be. But in the cross of our Savior, we are moving toward it. One day, the image of God will be fully restored in us.

Let that hope refresh and energize you as you meditate on the Scriptures, guided by this journal!

When you hear the word *delight*, do you imagine eating a dessert called "Death by Chocolate"? Do you picture yourself cracking the bedroom door to dote on your sleeping children or grandchildren? So what does the Bible mean when it says the Lord delights in us?

The Lord delights in me?

delight: please (someone) greatly
great pleasure

Apparently I please God. Huh? I feel almost more lost than ever trying to figure out how to best serve Him yet that, I guess makes sense, pleases Him.

The LORD delighteth in thee. Isaiah 62:4

The Person in the Mirror

Next time you glimpse yourself in the mirror, remember: "The Lord delights in me!" Then linger a moment, savoring the joy that awareness brings.

A thing is worth what someone will pay for it. Your heavenly Father redeemed you—bought you back for himself. The cost? The life of his beloved Son, Jesus Christ. Write a sentence or two about your struggles with self-worth. How does Romans 5:8 show you your worth in God's eyes and settle those concerns forever?

God commendeth his love toward us, in that, while we were yet sinners, Christ died for us.

Romans 5:8

Seeing through Jesus' Eyes

Put on your "Jesus glasses" as you interact with others. Ask your Savior to help you see that clerk at the mall, your supervisor, the bus driver, your kids' coach through his eyes of compassion and love.

When you imagine Jesus looking at you, do you feel unsettled? Or do you feel a quiet peace? Why do you think that might be? Talk to him about that now as you write, keeping Numbers 6:26 in mind.

The LORD lift up his countenance upon thee, and give thee peace.
Numbers 6:26

As I Reflect

In Jesus, your Savior, you are
God's fully forgiven, favored child!
Be at peace today in that truth.

Your mirror reveals your image in one way. An X-ray, in a second way. A CAT-scan, in yet a third. Only God sees and knows everything about you. When you remember that your Lord sees you through the eyes of his delight because of what Jesus did for you, what thoughts and joys arise in your heart?

_____

_____

_____

_____

_____

_____

_____

_____

_____

Thou knowest my downsitting and mine up-rising, thou understandest my thought afar off. Thou compassest my path and my lying down, and art acquainted with all my ways. For there is not a word in my tongue, but, lo, O LORD, thou knowest it altogether.
Psalm 139:2–4

The Person in the Mirror

Someone has said, "A friend is someone who knows all about you—and loves you anyway." What a Friend **you** have in Jesus!

Write about a time Jesus displayed his patient love to you. Thank him for it.

Howbeit for this cause I obtained mercy, that in me first Jesus Christ might shew forth all longsuffering, for a pattern to them which should hereafter believe on him to life everlasting. 1 Timothy 1:16

Seeing through Jesus' Eyes

Think of a child who looks up to you, a co-worker who admires you, someone at church who respects you. How might you gently shift his or her focus to Jesus, the Savior who has shown you such patient love?

When it comes to gifts, children tend to wish for the latest, greatest toy. They'll soon realize that wise parents usually have something even better in mind. Which would you rather have from your Savior: The things your heart desires? Or the desires he most wants you to have? Why?

Delight thyself also in the LORD; and he shall give thee the desires of thine heart.
Psalm 37:4

As I Reflect

Think about one desire Jesus has placed in your heart. Let it bring you delight today.

When we are sick, sad, or in trouble, it's easy to think God has walked away, that he is uncaring or unavailable. The Bible tells another story entirely. We can count on his help, because he delights in us! How does that truth help you remain patient, calm, and courageous?

He brought me forth also into a large place: he delivered me, because he delighted in me.
2 Samuel 22:20

The Person in the Mirror

Look into a mirror. Whom do you see there? One rescued by Christ Jesus on Calvary's cross? Yes! And one in whom God now delights!

In Jesus, you are the subject of God's limitless forgiveness and love. He delights in you! In what ways does recognizing those truths broaden, widen, and deepen your prayers?

O Lord, I beseech thee, let now thine ear be attentive to the prayer of thy servant, and to the prayer of thy servants, who desire to fear thy name. Nehemiah 1:11

_____

_____

_____

_____

_____

_____

_____

_____

_____

Seeing through Jesus' Eyes

When you come to God in prayer, there is nobody who can ask, "Who let you in here?!" You are always welcome—in Jesus' name!

Just as our Lord delights in us, he encourages us as his children to delight in one another. What blessings do other sisters in Christ bring into your life? What benefits come from these relationships? List them here.

But to the saints that are in the earth, and to the excellent, in whom is all my delight.
Psalm 16:3

As I Reflect

Think of one
or two faithful sisters in Christ
whose lives and words encourage you.
Thank Jesus. Then thank them in
some small but special way.

Write a sentence or two about your respect, your "fear" of the Lord. Then write a sentence or two about the hope you have in his unwavering love and mercy. Both reverence and hope are gifts from God to his people—to you! How do you experience those gifts in your life? How do they bring you joy?

The LORD taketh pleasure in them that fear him, in those that hope in his mercy. Psalm 147:11

The Person in the Mirror

Look into a mirror. Who is that person? Someone loved by the Savior with a love that has never changed and will never change.

What will it be like to see Jesus face-to-face? Think about the promise of 1 Corinthians 13:12. Then write about it.

For now we see through a glass, darkly; but then face to face: now I know in part; but then shall I know even as also I am known.

1 Corinthians 13:12

Seeing through Jesus' Eyes

We look forward to seeing Jesus face-to-face, but he longs for that meeting even more! Try thinking about that experience through Jesus' eyes. What do you imagine?

Moses gathered offerings from the people to use in building the tabernacle. Some of the women donated mirrors they had brought with them from Egypt, mirrors made from the most valuable, most highly polished bronze available. What thoughts come to mind as you consider the women's sacrifice?

And he made the laver of brass, and the foot of it of brass, of the lookingglasses of the women assembling, which assembled at the door of the tabernacle of the congregation.

Exodus 38:8

As I Reflect

Self-forgetful, Jesus held nothing back as he offered himself up for you on the cross. How does his sacrifice of love for you make you want to love him more?

Jesus, our Savior, is our treasure. His forgiveness, compassion, and love are priceless! We keep this treasure in "earthen vessels"—our frail, human bodies. We may think of this as a disadvantage, but what are the benefits?

We have this treasure in earthen vessels, that the excellency of the power may be of God, and not of us. 2 Corinthians 4:7

The Person in the Mirror

Each time you look into the mirror today, remind yourself that those around you see Jesus' strength shining most brightly through the window of your weaknesses: *When I am weak, then I am strong.*

2 Corinthians 12:10

Originally, Ezekiel 16 applied to God's Old Testament people. Despite their sins, the Lord had rescued them from slavery in Egypt—and this is how he saw them! Now, we are God's people by faith in our Savior, Jesus—and this is how God sees us! What will you say to him about that?

Thou wast exceeding beautiful, and thou didst prosper into a kingdom. And thy renown went forth among the heathen for thy beauty: for it was perfect through my comeliness, which I had put upon thee, saith the Lord GOD.

Ezekiel 16:13–14

Seeing through Jesus' Eyes

You may doubt your royal beauty, but Jesus does not! Peter writes: "Ye are a chosen generation, a royal priesthood, an holy nation, a peculiar people; that ye should shew forth the praises of him who hath called you out of darkness into his marvellous light" (1 Peter 2:9).

Our Lord first spoke the words of Exodus 19 to Moses. They describe God's affection for his Old Testament people. His affection for us, his people today, is no less tender, no less fierce, no less caring. As you consider that, what words of worship spring to mind?

I bare you on eagles' wings, and brought you unto myself. Now therefore, if ye will obey my voice indeed, and keep my covenant, then ye shall be a peculiar treasure unto me above all people: for all the earth is mine.
Exodus 19:4–5

As I Reflect

How did God bring you to himself in Christ Jesus? Which person or church family did he use? How might you thank them this week?

Read Proverbs 31:25–26. Then reread it, pausing to reflect on each word or phrase. What insights do you gain from meditating on this passage in this way?

Strength and honour are her clothing; and she shall rejoice in time to come. She openeth her mouth with wisdom; and in her tongue is the law of kindness. Proverbs 31:25–26

The Person in the Mirror

As you consider "the virtuous woman" described in Proverbs 31:10 and following, which sister in Christ comes to mind? Why not invite her to meet you for coffee and tell her?

What does your name mean? Did you know you have another name, too? One given by your heavenly Father? *Hephzibah* means "My Delight Is in Her"! What will you say to your Lord about that?

Thou shalt be called Hephzibah.
Isaiah 62:4

Seeing through Jesus' Eyes

New names can bring about new attitudes and spark new ventures. What is your new name creating in your life? What possibilities might Jesus see?

Isaiah 61:3 paints three before-and-after pictures. Which of these is most meaningful to you personally? Write about that picture.

To appoint unto them that mourn in Zion, to give unto them beauty for ashes, the oil of joy for mourning, the garment of praise for the spirit of heaviness; that they might be called trees of righteousness, the planting of the LORD, that he might be glorified.
Isaiah 61:3

As I Reflect

Imagine yourself as a "tree of righteousness," anchored firmly, "the planting of the LORD." What confidence does that give you for living as a woman of faith?

If you and your life are a "letter" from Christ, to whom are you being sent? What will your attitudes, words, and actions communicate to those who receive you?

_____

_____

_____

_____

_____

_____

_____

_____

_____

_____

_____

_____

Ye are manifestly declared to be the epistle of Christ ministered by us, written not with ink, but with the Spirit of the living God; not in tables of stone, but in fleshy tables of the heart.
2 Corinthians 3:3

The Person in the Mirror

Just think!
The Holy Spirit
has been writing
on your heart.
As you look into
the mirror, what
do you "read"
there?
Thank him!

Loved. Called. That's you! Right now! How does that reminder bring peace to your heart? What other thoughts and feelings does Romans 1:7 spark for you?

To all that be in Rome, beloved of God, called to be saints: Grace to you and peace from God our Father, and the Lord Jesus Christ.
Romans 1:7

_____

_____

_____

_____

_____

_____

_____

_____

Seeing through Jesus' Eyes

You are (probably) not in Rome as you read this. So where are you? What might Jesus want to see you do there today as his messenger of grace and peace?

When God sees us, he sees—and approves—the new hearts he has created in us by faith in the Savior (Psalm 51:10). When you evaluate others, when are you most likely to focus only on their "outward appearance"? Why might you want to change that practice? How can you change that focus?

The LORD seeth not as man seeth; for man looketh on the outward appearance, but the LORD looketh on the heart.
1 Samuel 16:7

As I Reflect

As you reflect on
1 Samuel 16:7, ask yourself
if there's anyone you may have
misjudged in recent weeks or months.
How might you correct any negative
consequences that resulted?

True wisdom includes insights into life's real meaning and the ability to deal with life's problems in godly ways, relying on Jesus for forgiveness and salvation. As you look back over your life so far, what wisdom has your Lord taught, placing it in your "secret heart"?

_____

_____

_____

_____

_____

_____

_____

_____

_____

_____

_____

_____

_____

_____

_____

_____

Behold, thou desirest truth in the inward parts:
and in the hidden part thou shalt make
me to know wisdom. Psalm 51:6

The Person in the Mirror

As you look into the mirror, do you see a wise woman? The answer is yes, because, "The fear of the LORD is the beginning of wisdom: a good understanding have all they that do his commandments" (Psalm-111:10).

When we're in the pits, it's easy to think that God is punishing us. That is never true. Jesus carried all our sins to his cross—and left them there. He has thrown our guilt behind his back. How does that good news give you courage to face today's troubles?

_____

_____

_____

_____

_____

_____

_____

_____

_____

_____

_____

_____

_____

_____

_____

_____

_____

Thou hast in love to my soul delivered it from the pit of corruption: for thou hast cast all my sins behind thy back. Isaiah 38:17

_____

_____

_____

_____

_____

_____

_____

_____

Seeing through Jesus' Eyes

Your Savior died to win
your freedom from guilt and fear.
He has no intention of turning around
to search for reasons to condemn you.
Ask him to help you see yourself
as God's forgiven daughter
always!

Spend a few minutes writing about each of these words: *precious, honourable, loved.*

Since thou wast precious in my sight, thou hast been honourable, and I have loved thee.
Isaiah 43:4

As I Reflect

Which sister
in Christ would find the words
of Isaiah 43:4 refreshing today?
Find a way to share
them with her!

God knew Moses by name. He knows you by name,
too! He hears your prayers, just as he heard the prayers
Moses offered. In Jesus, you have found favor in heaven.
Reflect on this. Then write a poem, letter, or paragraph
in response.

_____

_____

_____

_____

_____

_____

_____

_____

_____

_____

_____

_____

*I will do this thing also that thou hast spoken:
for thou hast found grace in my sight, and I
know thee by name. Exodus 33:17*

The Person in the Mirror

Look back through this journal. Find a Bible verse that truly encourages you. Print it out on a sticky note and affix it to your mirror. Read it each morning as you remember God's love for you.

Each blessing described in this journal is yours because you are the Lord's redeemed. Jesus bought you back from sin and death by suffering and dying for you on the cross. List your fears below. Then cross them out one by one as you repeat, "I am redeemed!"

Fear not: for I have redeemed thee, I have called thee by thy name; thou art mine. Isaiah 43:1

_____

_____

_____

_____

_____

_____

_____

_____

_____

_____

Seeing through Jesus' Eyes

As you get ready for bed
each evening, remind yourself:
"I am redeemed. Jesus knows my name.
I belong to him."
Then sleep in peace.

If this book has made a difference in your life or if you have simply enjoyed it, we would like to hear from you. Your words will encourage us! If you have suggestions for us to consider as we create books like this in the future, please send those, too.

Send e-mail to editor@CTAinc.com and include the subject line: RFL7PJKJ

Write to Editorial Manager, Dept. RFL7PJKJ

CTA, Inc.

PO Box 1205

Fenton, MO 63026-1205

Or leave a product review at www.CTAinc.com (search RFL7PJKJ)